THIS JOURNAL BELONGS TO:

_____

I hope this little journal brings a bit of beauty and inspiration to your everyday life. If you love this product, would you please consider leaving a review where you purchased it? We are a small family business: Your feedback helps us spread the word about our products. Thank-you!

More Like Grace

-Find more to love at www.morelikegrace.com -